Getting to Know

Joshua Tree National Park

by Patty Knapp

**CHILDREN'S OUTDOOR LIBRARY
MOOSE, WYOMING**

To Dani & Richie

Copyright © 1996 by M.I. Adventure Publications. All rights reserved. No part of this book may be reproduced in any way, or by any means, without written permission except for in the case of brief quotations in a review.

Children's Outdoor Library, M.I. Adventure Publications,
P.O. Box 277, Moose, WY 83012
Printed in Hong Kong

ISBN 0-9616395-6-3

Library of Congress Catalog Card Number: 95-69042

TABLE OF CONTENTS

WELCOME TO JOSHUA TREE NATIONAL PARK	5
THE JOSHUA TREE	6
PLENTY OF PLANTS	9
TWO DIFFERENT DESERTS	15
OASES	16
ADAPTABLE ANIMALS	18
MINI MYSTREY: SHILO'S DILEMMA	23
ROCK FORMATIONS AND GEOLOGY	24
INDIANS, COWBOYS, AND PIONEERS	28
CREATION OF A PARK	32
A GREAT PLACE TO VISIT	34
ACTIVITY PAGES	39
NATURE NOTES	41
ANSWER PAGE	44
PHOTO KEEPSAKES	45
MAP: JOSHUA TREE NATIONAL PARK	46
GLOSSARY / INDEX	48

Art Credits:
"Fact or Fiction" cartoons (pg. 6, 7, 9, 16, 19, 20, 27, 29, 31, 32, 35) and page 8 drawing - Jackie Czapla; page 29 drawing - T.J. Lee

Acknowledgements

Thanks to the staff of Joshua Tree National Park, members of the Joshua Tree National Park Association, students and teachers of S.A.D. 60 Elementary Schools, and helpful friends and family. Special thanks to park staff - Art Webster, Rosie Petito, Jeff Ohlfs, Joe Zerke; to Mrs. Heidi Porter and Ms. Carol Marcotte and their Third/Forth Grade classes - Danielle, Tim, Crystal, Tyler, Amanda, Andy, Jonathan, Shannon, Steven, Meaghan, Alaina, Forrest, Jessica, Zachary, Care, Jonathan, Ashlee, Ryan, Tom, Jason; to Ms. Karen Jewett and Mr. Bill Fulford and their Fifth Grade classes - Robert Ryan, Justin, Nathan, Nicole, Shannon, Sarah Rose, Shane, Rommel, Wiomi, Ashley; to Mrs. King and Ms. Ingrid Porter and their Sixth Grade classes - Michael, Amy, Brian, Ian, Lilli, Elise, Kate, Kim, Nate, Josie, J.P., Melissa, Isaish, Molly, Corey, Lisa Kelly, Harold; and friends and family - Peggy Furbush, Mary Nutter, Caileen Nutter, and Mac.

WELCOME TO JOSHUA TREE NATIONAL PARK

In the middle of Southern California, there is a beautiful place called Joshua Tree National Park. This desert park has unique plants and spectacular rock formations. It is a great place to enjoy desert scenery and to discover desert plant and animal life.

The park is an interesting place to learn the history of the California Desert. You can find many reminders of this desert's past. And there is plenty of opportunity for having fun. The park is an excellent place for enjoying many types of recreation — sightseeing, exploring, camping, hiking, backpacking and much more.

If you have never been to Joshua Tree, you might envision a forest of trees. However, there are no forests in this park. In fact, there are relatively few trees. Then why is this park named after a tree?

What kind of plants and animals can live in this desert? What makes this place special? What can you expect to see or do when you visit Joshua Tree National Park?

This book will answer these questions and help you explore the park. You'll have fun as you discover and learn about the desert. You can record your discoveries in the nature log at the back of the book. Use the map on pages 46 and 47 to help guide you on your adventure. The green numbered circles found throughout the book refer to the locations marked on this map.

Throughout the book, there are several orange boxes. Read the first statement of each box and decide if it is fact or fiction. Then read the remaining paragraphs in the box. You might change your answer after reading the whole box. Keep track of how many "Fact or Fiction" questions you get right on your first guess. Compare your results to the Explorer Thermometer on the answer page.

Are you ready? Go explore and have fun.

THE JOSHUA TREE

What is a Joshua tree and what makes it so unique? If you travel to the center of the park, you will quickly recognize this unusual plant. It is much larger than other desert plants. It can grow to over forty feet in height. Its somewhat eerie, but graceful shape, is not easily overlooked nor forgotten.

The Joshua tree's unique shape is what prompted its name. In the mid 1800's, a group of Mormon pioneers traveled through the desert. On their way, they happened upon a stand of Joshua trees. According to legend, the pioneers thought the uplifted tree branches looked like arms. These arms beckoned the group to continue to a promised land. Was this a sign from the prophet Joshua? That's what the pioneers thought. And so they named the trees after the prophet.

Joshua tree blossoms

PHOTOS BY PATTY FURBUSH

FACT OR FICTION: A Joshua tree is not really a tree. It's a lily.

The Joshua tree is a giant yucca plant, a member of the lily family. The Joshua is also a tree, although a unique tree. A typical tree has a hard wood core and soft leaves or needles. That is not so for the Joshua tree. The Joshua has a soft fibrous core. Instead of soft leaves, the branches have stiff green blades. These blades can grow up to a foot in length. When the leaf blades die, they fold against the tree and create a brown shag.

As you travel through the park, look for the stiff leaves and shaggy branches of the Joshua tree. Notice how different the Joshuas look from trees found in other parts of the country. (Now you know the first statement is fiction and the second statement is fact.)

Joshua trees bloom early in the spring. In February, blossoms begin to appear on the ends of the branches. A large Joshua tree covered with creamy white blossoms is a beautiful sight. It also means a feast for wildlife. Ground squirrels, birds, and deer love to eat the flowers.

Check out the "Fact or Fiction" boxes and picture captions to learn more about this unique plant. With so much life surrounding this one desert plant, it is easy to understand how the park got its name.

FACT OR FICTION:
Yucca moths attack Joshua trees and keep them from blooming.

A decrease in Joshua tree blooms is due mostly to differences in rainfall and temperature. The Yucca Moth is a friend of the Joshua tree. In fact, this moth and the Joshua tree need each other. Working together, the Yucca Moth and the Joshua tree create new life.

The Yucca Moth *pollinates* the Joshua tree then lays her eggs in the flower. The pollen fertilizes the Joshua flowers so seeds can develop. After the flowers die, large seed pods enclose the tree seeds and moth eggs. Moth larvae hatch from the eggs and feed on the seeds. After the larvae eat, they drill holes in the pod. Both larvae and the remaining Joshua tree seeds escape through the holes.

The larvae will eventually transform into new moths. Seeds from the pod will create Joshua tree seedlings. Look for a Joshua tree seed pod on the ground. Find the holes in the pod where the moth larvae escaped. (Now you know the statement is fiction.)

The Covington Tree is the largest known Joshua tree in the park. It stands about 40 feet high and measures about 17 feet around the base. Look for it near the Covington Flats ⑫ Backcountry Board.

Many animals use the Joshua tree as a food source. The cactus wren ❶ is one of several birds that eat insects found in this tree. The Loggerhead shrike ❷ (a type of bird) uses the tree's spikes to store its lizard meals. Hawks ❸ and ravens use the Joshua tree for a perch. From this high point, they can look for food on the ground below.

    The Joshua tree also provides homes for animals. Woodpeckers ❹ drill their homes in the tree trunks. Screech owls ❺ sometimes move into abandoned woodpecker holes. Orioles ❻ build hanging nests beneath the branches. Woodrats ❼ gnaw off the spiked leaves. The rats use the spikes to arm their nests against their enemies.

PLENTY OF PLANTS

The Joshua tree is just one of many plants protected in the park. All the plants in the park have one thing in common. They have adapted to living in an area of little rain. The park only gets 4 to 8 inches of rain a year. That's not much water. So how do these plants live in this dry desert climate?

The plants survive because they find and conserve water in many ways. Many plants have extensive root systems. With more roots, they can collect more water when it does rain. Some plants send roots deep into the ground in search of water. The mesquite tree sends roots up to sixty feet below ground.

Some plants lose their leaves during dry spells. Without leaves, the plant does not need as much water. Other plants hold moisture in thick waxy leaves.

The Cactus Family is well known for its ability to conserve water. Cactuses store water in their fleshy stems. This allows them to stay healthy between rains.

The thought of a cactus brings to mind sharp prickers and spines. But did you know that many types of cactuses have colorful flowers? In the spring, beautiful blossoms cover these spiny plants.

The beavertail cactus is the brightest cactus in the park. Its three-inch flowers are a brilliant pink. This cactus got its name because the stems look like the tails of beavers.

There are many other types of showy cactuses in the park. Red flowers with green centers cover the Mojave mound cactus. Look for the prickly pear, pancake and old man cactuses with their large yellow blossoms. The calico cactus has large pinkish-purple flowers.

Some types of cactuses are not quite as colorful. They have other characteristics that make them unique. The teddy bear cholla (*choy'-yah*) grows tall and bushy. A covering of silvery spines gives this cholla a fuzzy, soft appearance. However, it is far from being soft. Each cactus spine has a barbed hook that can penetrate skin and clothing at the slightest touch. The spines stick in the skin so easily that it seems they

FACT OR FICTION: The beavertail cactus is the only cactus that does not have spines.

From a distance, the beavertail cactus looks harmless. However, thousands of tiny yellow spines cover this cactus. These detachable spines will easily penetrate skin or clothing that brushes against the beavertail. Because of their small size, the spines are difficult to remove. Be extra careful not to touch this plant. (Now you know the statement is fiction.)

are jumping off the plant. That's why this plant is sometimes called a jumping cholla. But don't worry, the spines don't really jump.

The best place to see the teddy bear cholla is in the Cholla Cactus Garden ㉑. Hundreds of these plants grow in this natural garden area. Remember to stay on the path and don't touch the cholla.

The largest cactus in the park is the <u>barrel</u> <u>cactus</u>. The stems often grow to a foot in diameter and three or more feet in height. Large, thick, red spines cover this cactus and make it easy to identify. In the spring, small yellow flowers grow between the spines at the top of cactus.

Some other showy plants include the Mojave yucca, the Parry nolina, and the ocotillo. The <u>Mojave</u> <u>yucca</u> is a close relative of the Joshua tree. Like the Joshua tree, it is covered with large, dagger-like leaf blades. These blades are much longer and thicker than those of the Joshua. The blades can grow to three feet long and are very rigid. In the spring, a one to two foot long stem may sprout above the plant. The stem contains a large bushy cluster of creamy white flowers.

The <u>Parry</u> <u>nolina</u> resembles the Mojave yucca. However, the leaves are longer and less rigid than those on a yucca. The flower stems can sprout up to five feet high and spread out to three feet in width. It's a spectacular sight.

The <u>ocotillo</u> (o-ko-tee'-yo) is an unusual plant that grows in the southern part of the park. The plant has clusters of long, skinny, thorn-covered stems. It commonly grows up to twelve feet in height. Through most of the year, the ocotillo is brown, leafless and looks dead. However, within a few days after a rain, the plant sprouts thousands of small leaves. The leaves cover the stems from the ground to the top of the plant. When the ocotillo blooms, bright red tubular blossoms brighten the end of each stem. Visit the Ocotillo Patch ㉒ to see a large group of these plants.

Rainy winters and mild spring temperatures help create spectacular wildflower displays. Under the right conditions, thousands of annual wildflowers speckle the desert with color. Purplish-pink <u>sand</u> <u>verbena</u> and white <u>dune</u> <u>primrose</u> grow in sandy soils. Bluish-purple <u>Canterbury</u> <u>bells</u> sprout from rocky hillsides. Thick daisy-sized brittlebush flowers and carpets of <u>desert</u> <u>dandelions</u> color the desert yellow. The <u>Mariposa</u> <u>lily</u> brightens stony soils with its three brilliant orange petals. The <u>sacred</u> <u>datura</u>'s large, white, trumpet blossom and the orange, cup-shaped blossoms of the <u>globemallow</u> decorate roadsides. Lavender <u>Mojave aster</u>, white desert lily, pink five-spot, purple phacelia, scarlet locoweed— the names and colors of spring wildflowers go on and on.

> Now that you have read about the plants above, try to match up their names with the pictures that follow. (Hint: Look for the underlined plants in the above text. They are the plants pictured.) Take a walk through the desert and see how many of these different plants you can find. Remember to record your findings in your nature notes at the end of the book.

Answers:

A. Parry Nolina
B. sand verbena, primrose
C. Mojave aster
D. barrel cactus
E. Mariposa lily
F. sacred datura
G. yucca, globemallow
H. ocotillo
I. teddy bear cholla
J. calico cactus
K. Mojave mound cactus
L. Canterbury bells
M. beavertail
desert dandylion

C. _____

D. _____

A. _____

B. _____
_____
_____

E. _____
F. _____

G. _____
_____
H. _____

I.

J.

K.

PHOTOS BY PATTY FURBUSH

L.

M.

13

Above: Carpets of spring wildflowers color the Colorado Desert.
Right: Joshua trees, yuccas, and cholla are common plants in the Mojave Desert.

TWO DIFFERENT DESERTS

There are two deserts in the park. They are the Colorado and Mojave (moh-hah'-vee) Deserts. A trip to Joshua Tree National Park provides an opportunity to explore these two different deserts.

The Mojave Desert is called the high desert. It lies at elevations over 2000 feet above sea level. Much of the northern and western parts of the park are in the Mojave. The Colorado Desert is the low desert. It lies at elevations less than 3000 feet. It covers most of the southern and eastern parts of the park. The two deserts overlap in an area called the Transition Zone. Look at the map on pages 46 & 47 to locate these three desert areas.

The Mojave Desert has the cooler and wetter climate of the two deserts. As a result, the vegetation is thicker. Look for the Joshua tree. It's the most telltale sign of being in the Mojave Desert. Joshua trees only grow at elevations over 3000'. Other large plants in the Mojave Desert include pinyon pine and juniper. These trees grow throughout the rugged mountains. Look for them along the roads to Keys View ⑩ and Covington Flats ⑫.

The Colorado Desert is dryer and warmer than the Mojave Desert. Vegetation is sparse. However, there are many different kinds of trees. Mesquite, palo verde, and smoke trees grow along the washes. A plant that signals being in the Colorado Desert is the ocotillo. Watch for this tall, spindly, multi-stemmed plant.

Travel from Pinto Wye ⑲ to Pinto Basin to see the differences in the two deserts. Pinto Wye is in the Mojave Desert. Pinto Basin is in the Colorado Desert. Notice the many Joshua trees around Pinto Wye. As you travel through Pinto Basin, you will pass through the park's largest known ocotillo patch ㉒.

PHOTOS BY PATTY FURBUSH

OASES

There are five oases in the park. An oasis is a group of plants surrounding a natural desert water source. Grasses, cottonwoods, and willows grow in the moist oasis soil. Groves of native California fan palms tower above the other oasis plants. In some oases, water forms pools or trickles on the surface. In other oases, the water is underground. All of the park oases provide water, food, and homes for many birds and animals.

The largest oasis is in a rugged canyon in the south part of the park. A four and one-half mile trail leads through rolling hills from Cottonwood to Lost Palms Oasis ㉔.

A shorter, more strenuous trail leads to Fortynine Palms Oasis ②. This one and one-half mile trail leads over a ridge then down into Fortynine Palms Canyon. Over the years, several fires have burned this area leaving palm trees with black trunks. There are boulders and pools of water beneath the palm tree canopy. Sit on one of the boulders and listen. How many different sounds can you hear?

FACT OR FICTION: Fires can be good for palm trees.

Palm trees sprout new leaves soon after a fire. The burned trees usually produce more seeds than they produced before the fire. With more seeds there will be more palm tree seedlings.

Oasis fires kill mesquite trees. Palm trees benefit from the burning of mesquite in two ways. Mesquite trees consume much water. Without the mesquite, there is more water for palms. And with the bushy mesquites gone, more sunlight can reach palm tree seedlings.

Long ago, Native Americans frequently set palm trees on fire and burned the oases. They burned to rid the trees of insects. Because of the frequent burning, the oases were open and grassy. There were very few shrubs.

These early people have long since left the oases. The frequent fires have stopped. Smaller plants and trees have created a thick underbrush. If a wildfire burned through an oasis today, the intense heat could kill the palm trees.

To prevent this danger, the National Park Service occasionally conducts controlled burns. They clear out the underbrush by burning small sections of an oasis. During the burns, firefighters keep the fire from getting out of control. (Now you know the statement is fact.)

A hiker enjoys Lost Palms Canyon 24.

The Oasis of Mara 1 (also called Twentynine Palms Oasis) and Cottonwood Spring 23 are the easiest oases to visit. Both oases are near parking areas. A nature trail leads through each area. Signs and pamphlets explain how important these areas were to early Native Americans and pioneers.

17

ADAPTABLE ANIMALS

Are the deserts of Joshua Tree National Park too hot and dry for animals? Indeed, there is not much water in the park. And summers can be very hot with temperatures climbing above 110° F. However, many different types of animals have *adapted* to living in this desert climate.

Some animals such as the bobcat, fox, and kangaroo rat are *nocturnal*. They only come out in the cooler evening and at night. Desert birds cool themselves on hot days by rapidly moving air in their throats. Desert iguanas can tolerate high body temperatures up to 115°F. Compare that to human body temperatures. Humans only tolerate body temperatures up to 106° F.

Snakes and lizards have scaly skin. Their skin protects them from heat and helps them conserve water. Insects have hard outer shells that prevent water loss.

Animals like the ground squirrel, the roadrunner, and red-tailed hawk have learned to survive without drinking water. They get their water from the plants, insects, or animals they eat. Toads survive without water by burying themselves in soil or hiding in

Coyotes are commonly seen in the park. They roam both day and night. In the evening, listen for their barks and yips followed by long howls. Coyotes are very adaptable. They will eat anything from plants to *carrion.*

GARY W. JEFFERSON

FACT OR FICTION: The kangaroo rat can go its entire life without a drink of water.

The Kangaroo Rat gets its water from the food it eats. As it digests its food, this animal *metabolizes* additional water inside its body. The Kangaroo rat only comes out at night when it is cooler and not quite as dry. This conserves moisture and reduces the rat's need for water. (Now you know the statement is fact.)

deep rock crevices. They stay buried until it rains.

Some desert animals must drink water to survive. However, even these animals have adapted to living in a dry environment. The desert tortoise has body parts that store water. The tortoise needs to drink only once or twice a year. A desert bighorn sheep can travel three or four days before it needs water.

About eighty species of reptiles, amphibians, and mammals make their home in the park. Over 200 species of birds frequent the park. The best way to see the park's wildlife is to walk or sit quietly away from the high traffic areas.

Although wildlife is abundant in the desert, it is not easy to spot. Many of the animals have *camouflage* coloring. They blend in with the desert. Some animals move very quickly from one hiding place to another. Others sit very still to avoid being seen. Often it is easier to hear the animals than to see them. Listen for the howl of the coyote, the shrill call of a hawk, or the hoot of an owl.

As you travel through the park, look and listen. Try to identify some of the animals. These pictures will help you. Record your findings in your nature notes at the end of the book.

The horned lizard protects itself from *predators* in many ways. Its *camouflage* coloring allows it to blend in with the desert soil. This lizard is very difficult to spot.

A horned lizard can squirt blood from its eye to startle its predator. Spiked scales cover the lizard's head and body. What an unpleasant meal for any snake who tries to sample this lizard.

NATIONAL PARK SERVICE

19

PATTY FURBUSH

Desert bighorn sheep are shy and nervous. They prefer isolated places and steep, rugged terrain. Their sponge-like feet help them move with ease over rocky ground.

Every few days, the bighorn must make a quick trip to a water hole. They have a special ability to drink quickly and *rehydrate* in minutes. They can get in and out of a water hole before predators discover they are there.

JIM TALLON

The red-tailed hawk is the park's most frequently seen *bird of prey*. Look for this impressive bird soaring in the air or perched on top of a Joshua tree.

This hawk has a five foot wingspan. It can dive down through the air at speeds up to 100 mph. The high speed dive makes it easy for the hawk to catch its prey.

FACT OR FICTION:
The roadrunner can run 50 MPH.

Indeed, this bird can run fast. However, the roadrunner's tornado-like speeds exist only in cartoons. The roadrunner's top speed is estimated at 18 miles per hour. (Now you know the statement is fiction.)

GARY W. JEFFERSON

The mountain lion lives in isolated areas. It is seldom seen. The lion roams day and night, covering up to 20 miles a day. It preys upon small or weak animals.

A lion can weigh up to 160 pounds, grow up to 5 feet long, and stand three feet high. Amazingly, it can jump 15 feet from the ground up to a perch. That's about the height of a building's second story window.

The bobcat is mainly *nocturnal*. At night, it hunts for small animals, birds, and snakes. In the day, it dozes.

Listen for the bobcat's loud screams, hisses, and other eerie sounds during evenings. Late winter is the bobcat's mating season. During this time, bobcats are the most vocal.

The black-tailed jackrabbit is active in the early morning and evening. This hare is easy to identify by its huge ears. The large ears help the jackrabbit remove excess body heat. The large ears also alert the jackrabbit to *predators*.

The jackrabbit can make a quick escape by leaping distances of over 20 feet. (How many leaps does it take you to cover 20 feet?)

The sidewinder or horned rattlesnake is one type of snake that lives in the park. It has a unique way of moving its body by making sideways, looping "S" curves. Special scales above the eyes give this snake a horned appearance.

Rattlesnakes are poisonous but they are not aggressive. Avoid an encounter by watching where you walk. The snakes in this park hibernate during the winter, usually from November to March.

The roadrunner prefers to run rather than fly. It makes quick darting movements to catch its *prey*. The roadrunner dines on lizards, rodents, insects, scorpions, and snakes. Look for the roadrunner's unique "X" shaped footprint on sandy ground.

Look for the desert tortoise when weather is warm. During winter cold and extreme summer heat, this tortoise *hibernates* in burrows.

The desert tortoise stores large amounts of water in its bladder. If someone picks up a tortoise, the tortoise may become frightened. It may expel the stored water. Without the water, the tortoise may die of *dehydration*.

The tiny antelope ground squirrel is active in mid day. Look for it perched on a yucca or scurrying over boulders. Its small size, quick movements, and flickering tail make him easy to identify. This squirrel is only about 4 inches long, not counting its tail.

The largest lizard in the park is the chuckwalla. It commonly grows to a foot in length and four inches in width.

The chuckwalla has a unique way of protecting itself. When frightened, it crawls into a crack and inflates itself by filling its lungs with air. *Predators* can't remove the wedged lizard from the crack.

It is easy to identify a quail. Look for the feather plume on top of this bird's head.

Gambel's quail usually travel in coveys of 4-40 birds. When startled by *predators* or hikers, the quail fly off in all different directions. This flurry of activity startles predators and allows the birds time to escape. (Do you think you will jump the first time you come across a flurry of quail?)

Don't be scared by the huge, hairy tarantula. This gentle spider has no interest in biting people. It uses its large fangs and mild poison to catch and digest its insect *prey*.

MINI MYSTERY: SHILO'S DILEMMA

Test your detective skills. Read the story below. See if you can solve the mystery.

Shilo moved slowly but steadily up the rocky hillside. She was very thirsty. "I shouldn't have waited so long to get a drink of water," she thought to herself. "It's been over four days since I've had a drink."

Although Shilo was dehydrated, she was still able to move with ease over the large boulders. Near the top of the mountain, she came across a high sloping cliff. There was no way around it. Without pausing, she ran toward the cliff. Then with a leap, she jumped onto the rock face. Her feet seemed to stick to the rock like suction cups to glass. In a matter of seconds, she was up the cliff and continuing on her way.

The sun was setting as Shilo reached the top of the mountain.

"I'm glad I'm done climbing," thought Shilo. "I'm too thirsty to climb that again."

Shilo looked down the other side of the mountain. There, a short distance below, was the pond and the water she needed so desperately. Next to the pond, something orange flapped in the evening breeze.

"What's that?" wondered a nervous Shilo as she dashed behind a boulder.

Cautiously, she peeked below. Three people were moving about near the orange object. Shilo stayed hidden and listened to their voices.

"Dad, this is a great camp spot. Do you think we will see any wildlife?" asked a small boy voice.

An older man voice answered. "Let's sit quietly next to this rock. Surely, we'll see some wildlife."

"Oh what are these people doing here?" sighed Shilo. "Don't they know it's getting late? Soon it will be dark."

She looked longingly at the water below. "I'm so thirsty. But I will have to wait or go somewhere else for a drink of water."

Shilo was trying to decide what to do when she heard the third voice.

"Dad! Quick, pack up. We can't stay here! Look at this information I got from the Ranger," exclaimed a small girl voice. "This map shows we are in a day use area."

"Let's see," said the man.

After a short while, the man spoke again. "You're right Daisy. Let's pack up and move. If we hurry, we can get out of the day use area before dark."

"What's the big deal?" asked the boy.

"Day use areas are set aside to benefit wildlife," answered the man. "If we stay here at night, we will keep thirsty animals from getting a drink. Come on. I'll tell you all about it as we hike."

Within a matter of minutes, the three voices faded away down the canyon. Shilo slipped out from behind the boulder. She used her sharp senses to check the area over. She decided it was safe then moved cautiously but rapidly down to the water's edge.

She dipped her face into the pond and took a long, long drink. "Water never tasted so good," thought Shilo.

Within a few minutes, Shilo finished drinking. She felt great. She bounded back up the hillside with renewed strength. "Day use areas are wonderful," thought Shilo as she disappeared into the rugged hills.

1. Who or what is Shilo? 2. Where in the park do you think you might find Shilo? 3. How can Shilo climb so easily over rocky terrain? 4. Why did the voices leave?

Answers: page 44

23

ROCK FORMATIONS AND GEOLOGY

The gigantic boulder formations in the park are a beautiful but curious sight. Did these piles of rock push up from the hillsides and valley floor? Or did some powerful force roll these large boulders into piles?

The rock piles were formed underground. Millions of years ago, molten liquid oozed upward from the inner earth. The liquid cooled and crystallized below the ground. This formed a rock called monzogranite. The ground containing the monzogranite gradually shifted upward bringing the rock closer to the surface (*Figure 1*).

Ground water filtered down through the soil and seeped into cracks in the monzogranite. The water created a chemical reaction that changed the edges of the rock into soft clay (*Figure 2*). Erosion stripped away the old ground surface exposing the monzogranite. Wind and water removed the soft

In the northwest part of the park, there is an area called the Wonderland of Rocks ④. This twelve square mile area is a maze of jumbled rock formations. It's an amazing sight. Roads lead through the outer edge of the Wonderland at Hidden Valley and Indian Cove. You can hike into the Wonderland on the Barker Dam ⑥ and Hidden Valley ⑦ nature trails.

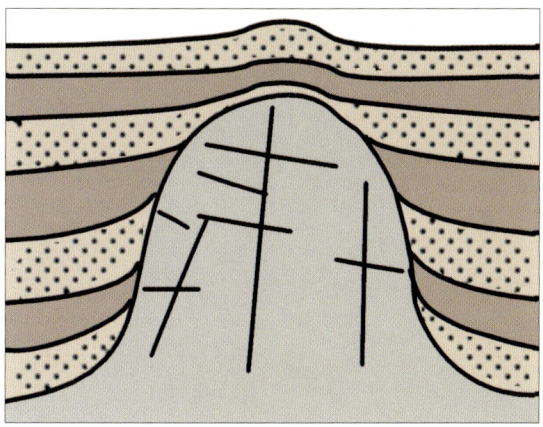

Figure 1

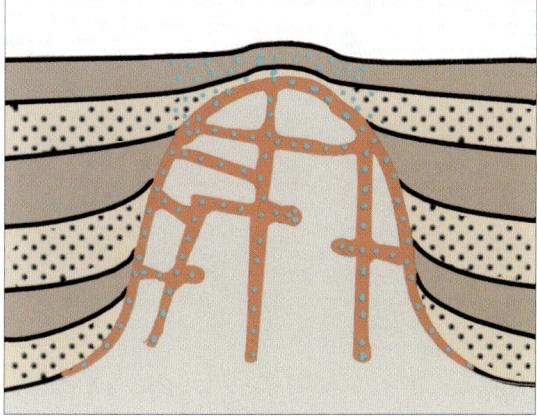

Figure 2

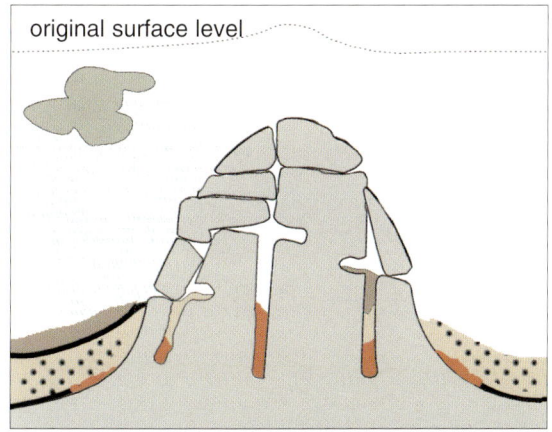

Figure 3

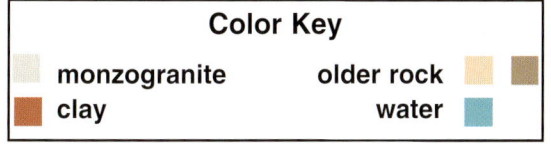

Look for the "Trojan" along the Hidden Valley Nature Trail 7. This head-shaped rock is on the right side near the start of the loop.

clay covering the rocks. As the clay eroded from the cracks, large rounded boulders collapsed into piles (*Figure 3*).

Use your imagination to see the many shapes and figures in the boulder piles. Look for the "Old Woman" *(pg. 4)* and "Cyclops" formations in Hidden Valley Campground. The "Trojan" and the "Ox" are along the Hidden Valley Nature Trail 7. Near Belle Campground, you'll find "Bread Loaf Rock." The most well known formation, "Skull Rock" 16 is near Jumbo Rocks Campground. Skull Rock is shaped like a gigantic human skull.

Look for the "Cap Rock" and "Headstone Rock" formations and see if you can guess how they got their names. Cap Rock ⑧ is on the road to Keys View ⑩. Headstone Rock is in Ryan Campground.

Joshua Tree National Park has many other interesting geologic features. There are sand dunes in Pinto Basin and a *slot canyon* in Indian Cove ③.

Ride down the Geology Tour Road ⑱ to learn more about the geology of the park. A booklet, available at the start of the road, explains the sixteen geologic stops. (Obtain information on road conditions before attempting this drive.)

A one mile walk in Pinto Basin leads to the sand dunes at the base of Pinto Mountain.

PHOTOS BY PATTY FURBUSH

Wind and water went to work on some rock piles and created natural rock arches. A short trail in White Tank Campground leads to the best known arch in the park — Arch Rock [20]. The arch spans a 35 foot distance. Signs along the trail explain how the arch formed. (If you explore the rocks, be careful and make sure an adult is with you. Stay close to the ground. Falls from rock piles can cause serious injuries.)

FACT OR FICTION:

Malapai Hill is an extinct volcano that rises from the center of the park. *(Park Map Locator # 17.)*

About 2-3 million years ago, liquid rock pushed up from the inner earth. If the molten rock had reached the surface, there would have been a volcano or lava flow. However, it stopped below the ground surface and formed a hard rock plug. Over time, the ground surrounding the plug eroded away. Look for this rock plug, known as Malapai Hill, on the Geology Tour Road. It stands alone, rising 400 feet above the valley floor. (Now you know the statement is fiction.)

INDIANS, COWBOYS, AND PIONEERS

A couple hundred years ago, Native Americans were the only people in the California Desert. The Cahuilla (kah-wee'-yah), Chemehuevi, and Serrano Indians traveled through the area looking for food. They hunted sheep, antelope, and small animals such as lizards and rabbits. They gathered the buds, fruits, and seeds of many desert plants.

These tribes had other uses for plants and animals besides food. They used animal skins for clothing. From yucca fibers, they made baskets, sandals, and bow strings. Palm leaves provided material for building houses and making twine.

These Indians were seasonal hunters and gatherers. They frequented the park area during the winter months. They traveled from campsite to campsite looking for food and water. When they moved from a campsite, they sometimes left some of their belongings. These items included arrow points, pottery, and baskets.

Park *archaeologists* have collected these items, which they call artifacts. By studying these artifacts, archaeologists can learn about the life of these early people. The National Park Service preserves most of the artifacts in the park museum. Look for some artifacts on display at the Oasis Visitor Center ❶.

A bedrock mortar is one reminder of early human life that you can see while hik-

The Serrano Indians sometimes left baskets and pottery in their abandoned campsites. Archaeologists can learn about these early people by studying artifacts like these.

ing. A mortar is a hole in the rock where early American Indians ground seeds and nuts. Hike the short nature trail at Cottonwood Spring ㉓ to see some mortars.

The first white settlers came to the area in the late 1800's. Some of these settlers grazed cattle. In those days, grass was more abundant than it is in the park today.

Two of the first cowboys in the area were Jim and Bill McHaney. The McHaney brothers were suspected of rustling (stealing) cattle. According to local legend, the McHaneys hid stolen cattle in an area known as Hidden Valley. The rocky hills surrounding the valley formed a natural corral. Visit this area by hiking the Hidden Valley Nature Trail ⑦. The trail enters the valley through a narrow gap in the rocks. It is easy to see how the McHaneys could have kept the cattle hidden.

FACT OR FICTION:

Pictographs and petroglyphs are two kinds of prehistoric Native American art.

Prehistoric American Indians often painted red designs on rocks and boulders. A few of these designs, called pictographs, are still visible today. Sometimes Indians chipped or carved pictures into dark rock surfaces. Archaeologists call these designs petroglyphs. Some archaeologists believe that pictographs and petroglyphs may have been a form of communication. To view some petroglyphs, hike the Barker Dam Nature Trail. (Now you know the statement is fact.)

However, water was scarce. Then how did the cattle find enough to drink?

Ranchers and cowboys built small dams in many desert washes. Rain water collected behind the walls and created watering holes for the cattle. Today, most of the these watering holes have dried up and filled with sand. However, one of the largest watering holes still holds water. Hike the Barker Dam Nature Trail 6 to see the small lake behind Barker Dam.

Some early desert settlers found gold. This brought many prospectors to the area. The gold miners built mines, mills, and small towns throughout the desert. A few of the mines in the park produced a wealth of gold. The Lost Horse and the Desert Queen were two of these mines.

The Desert Queen Mine 15 was one of the richest mines in the area. It produced gold worth several million dollars. A short trail leads to an overlook of this area. You can see machinery and mine shafts on the hillside below the overlook.

One of the most interesting pioneers in the area was Bill Keys. Bill was a young man when he settled in the area in 1910. He made his living by doing a little bit of everything. He did farming, ranching, mining, and milling.

Bill raised a family on the Desert Queen Ranch 5. The ranch was in a rocky canyon, fifty miles from the nearest town. Fifty miles was too far to go for groceries and supplies. So the Keys family took care of most of their needs at the ranch. They grew crops and fruit trees and raised cattle. Mr. and Mrs. Keys even opened a schoolhouse for their children.

When Bill Keys died in 1969, the National Park Service took over the ranch. Today the Park Service preserves the ranch.

Miners built a large ten-stamp mill at the Lost Horse Mine 9. A mill is a structure used to crush and process the gold-bearing rock. Hike the two mile trail to the Lost Horse Mine to see this mill. (For a shorter hike to a mill, ask a ranger about the Wall Street Mill.)

Go on a guided tour of the Desert Queen Ranch ⑤ and learn about the life of the Keys family. Imagine being a pioneer living in this isolated, rocky, desert canyon.

FACT OR FICTION:

In the early 1900's, Bill Keys operated a recycling center at the Desert Queen Ranch.

Bill Keys did not call the Desert Queen Ranch a recycling center. However, the definition does fit. Keys tried to reuse everything he could. He acquired equipment from abandoned mines in the area. He stored this equipment in organized piles on the ranch. When he needed to fix something, he would look in his piles. Hopefully, he would find just the right part.

Mr. Keys had many uses for his recycled equipment. He made a chicken coop out of a large mining tank. And he turned a tractor into a wood cutting machine.

For Bill Keys, getting supplies at a store meant riding 50 miles over rough dirt roads. That took a long time traveling by horse or early motorcar. Bill Keys saved much time and money by recycling everything he could. (Now you know the statement is fact.)

CREATION OF A PARK

In the early 1900's, the Southern California Desert was a quiet but beautiful place. There was an abundance of desert plants growing throughout the area. There were very few visitors.

As the years went on, more and more people came to the desert to view its natural beauty. Many people enjoyed the plants so much that they took the plants home to their gardens. Unfortunately, people removed the plants much faster than nature could replace them.

Some people set Joshua trees on fire. The blazing plants provided light as visitors traveled through the area at night. However, the fires killed the Joshua trees. Nature is slow to replace these unique plants.

As a result of these activities, desert plants rapidly disappeared. A concerned citizen, Mrs. Minerva Hoyt, realized that the desert was losing its natural beauty. She began a crusade to save the desert. Her work led her to Washington D.C. where she met with the President of the United States. The President agreed wholeheartedly with her proposal to protect the California Desert.

In 1936, President Franklin D. Roosevelt established Joshua Tree National Monument. The area was named after the Joshua tree, the largest and most unusual plant in the monument. Many years later, Congress decided that this desert area deserved recognition as a park. In 1994, Congress passed a bill creating Joshua Tree National Park.

FACT OR FICTION:

The main purpose of a national monument is to protect large statues or buildings.

National Park Service areas get their title according to how they are created. Only Congress has the power to create a national park. However, the President of the United States can use a presidential proclamation to create a national monument.

Many national monuments protect natural areas that don't have statues or buildings. Both parks and monuments receive the same federal protection. (Now you know the statement is fiction.)

An occasional snowfall adds to the beauty of the park's back roads.

A GREAT PLACE TO VISIT

Begin your visit to the park at the Oasis Visitor Center ① in Twentynine Palms. There you will find exhibits on the wildlife, plants, geology, and history of the park. You can watch a film or talk to a ranger about what to see and do.

Driving through the park is one way to explore and learn about the park. Roads wind through interesting rock formations and travel through the different plant communities. Some roads lead to spectacular view points. Keys View ⑩ is one of these points. Keys View sits on the crest of the Little San Bernardino Mountains. From the overlook, you can see the Coachella Valley and the distant Salton Sea. On a clear day, you can even see as far as Mexico.

For the more adventurous, there are dirt roads. The Covington Flats Road leads to the top of Eureka Peak ⑬. From Eureka Peak, you can see low desert valleys and high mountains. Look for the two towering mountains that rise over 10,000 feet in elevation. These mountains are Mt. San Jacinto to the south and Mt. San Gorgonio to the west.

Many people come to Joshua Tree to camp. One of the great things about camping in the desert is the weather. Temperatures are

Rock boulder piles and nearby trails make it fun to explore around the campgrounds.

pleasant in the spring, fall, and most of the winter. There is very little rain and the sky is often clear and blue. However, sometimes it does get cold, wet, or windy. Even though the weather is usually great, campers should be prepared for unpleasant weather.

There are eight campgrounds in the park. Some campgrounds have amphitheaters where rangers give programs. You can watch a slide program about the park or sit around a campfire and talk with a ranger.

Hiking is one of the best ways to explore Joshua Tree. Park Rangers lead several hikes. On these hikes, the ranger will talk about the park's natural history.

There are many fun places to hike without a ranger, too. Nature trails lead through interesting and weird rock formations or to impressive lookout points. One nature trail leads to a desert lake formed behind Barker Dam ⑥. Another leads to a big rock archway, Arch Rock ⑳. Signs along the trails tell about the plants, animals, geology, and history of the area.

The California Riding & Hiking Trail ⑪ travels 35 miles from the west side of the park to the northeast side of the park. Both horseback riders and hikers enjoy using the trail.

There are also longer trails in the park. These trails lead to beautiful oases like Lost Palms ㉔ and Fortynine Palms ②. Some trails lead to the top of mountains such as Ryan Mountain ⑭ and Inspiration Peak ⑩. Historic ruins like Lost Horse Mine ⑨ and Wall Street Mill are at the end of other trails.

FACT OR FICTION: Rock climbing is a very dangerous sport.

If you don't have the proper training or equipment, rock climbing can be very dangerous. Many untrained people have been seriously hurt while trying to climb.

Trained climbers attach themselves to a special rope. They climb by putting their hands and feet into cracks or on rock edges. As they go up, they place climbing hardware in the cracks. They clip their rope through each of these man-made anchor points. If a climber slips, the rope and hardware keep him from falling to the ground. Climbing with training and the proper equipment makes the sport of rock climbing much safer. (Now you know the statement can be both fact and fiction.)

Some hikers go on overnight backpacking trips. Camping away from roads is a great way to experience the peaceful desert.

Rock climbers come to the park in search of a physical challenge. They come from all over the world to climb Joshua Tree's rock formations. If you visit the park in spring or fall, you will see these agile visitors scaling steep-sided rocks. The best place to view these athletes is at Hidden Valley Campground. Many of the climber's favorite boulder piles are in Hidden Valley.

Below: The Hidden Valley Trail ⑦ is one of twelve self-guiding nature trails in the park. Left: Trained rock climbers are challenged by the parks many boulder piles.

A great way to experience the park is to find a quiet place to relax. Just sit, look, and listen. Discover this wonderful desert.

Joshua Tree National Park covers over 1000 square miles. That's bigger than the state of Rhode Island. That's too big to explore in a short trip. But you can return to Joshua Tree again and again. You can explore new areas and new wonders each time you come. Whether you come for a week or just a day, you'll have fun getting to know this special desert park.

Joshua Tree National Park has been preserved so everyone can enjoy this special place. We can be thankful that Mrs. Minerva Hoyt organized her crusade to save this area. Now it's up to you. Go enjoy and discover Joshua Tree National Park. But be sure to take good care of it. Remember this is your desert. This is your National Park!

Word Search: Desert Life

Answer the following clues about the plants and animals in the park. Then circle your answers in the word search puzzle. The answers to the clues can be found in the word list at the bottom of the page. All the plants and animals in the word list are in the word search puzzle. To make the puzzle more challenging, try to answer the clues without looking at the word list.

1. This animal is commonly seen in the park. It is related to the domestic dog. _____
2. This plant can sprout flower stems up to 5 feet in height and 3 feet in width. _____
3. This animal's small size, quick movements, and flickering tail make it easy to identify. It is only about 4 inches in size. _____ _____
4. The park is named after this plant. _____ _____
5. The sidewinder is one of several types of _____ found in the park. It has special scales above its eyes that look like horns.
6. The largest lizard in the park can inflate with air and wedge itself in a crack. _____
7. It is large, hairy, and has fangs. However, it is very gentle. _____
8. Look for the plume feather on this bird's head. _____
9. This large white trumpet is not an instrument; it's a flower. _____
10. The largest animal in the park is the mountain _____.
11. The largest cactus in the park has red spines and small yellow flowers. _____
12. Don't pick up this slow moving animal. It may expel the water stored in its bladder. The loss of water may cause this animal to die of dehydration. _____

Answers: page 44

```
C A L I C O C A C T U S H W T P R L Z L S H M D
T O R T O I S E D E E R F R A A A J D I H T R A
A S T E R G R O U N D S Q U I R R E L O R I A N
J O S H U A T R E E L Y J L I L Y A R N I S P D
V E R B E N A R Q R T W Z N C Z J S N A K E S E
B A R R E L F L S U J V K G H H Y V F T E B H L
V F O X N O L I N A A C X N O L O W N T U I J I
H S M O J A V E J P R I M R O S E L Y Q F L S O
C H U C K W A L L A R G L O B E M A L L O W A N
X C O Y O T E O W L J P A M D A T U R A W R E N
```

WORD LIST

coyote	chuckwalla	barrel	deer	globemallow
tortoise	tarantula	shrike	aster	owl
ground squirrel	Joshua tree	quail	lily	wren
lion	nolina	verbena	fox	cholla
snakes	datura	calico cactus	primrose	dandelion

Crossword Puzzle: Park Facts

Down:

2. Two different species of this animal live in the park. They are the Kangaroo _____ and Wood _____.
4. The name of a cactus that has bright pink flowers.
6. This plant is a close relative of the Joshua tree
10. To explore the park and trails on foot
11. This is another name for the teddy bear cholla.
13. This plant sprouts new leaves a few days after it rains.
15. This lizard can squirt blood from its eye.
17. The name of the Desert Queen Ranch family

Across:

1. The name of the pioneers that gave the Joshua tree its name
3. This cat comes out at night to hunt.
5. The lady who began the crusade to protect the area now know as Joshua Tree National Park
7. Another name for Twentynine Palms Oasis
8. The name of the rock formation where you will find the park's largest arch.
9. These birds build hanging nests in Joshuas.
11. This animal can leap over 20 feet when it is trying to escape from a predator.
12. The rock formations are composed of this type of rock.
14. A hole in the rock where early American Indians ground seeds.
15. This bird can dive through the air at speeds up to 100 mph.
16. This is another name for the Low Desert.
18. This bird prefers to run rather than fly.
19. You'll find many of these scaly-skinned animals in the park.

Answers: page 44

Nature Notes

Explorer's Checklist: Keep track of your discoveries. Your notes will help you remember your visit. If you come back to the park, your notes might help you refind a special place.

Animals:	Date	Location	Observations
☐ bighorn sheep			
☐ bobcat			
☐ cactus wren			
☐ chuckawalla			
☐ collard lizard			
☐ cottontail rabbit			
☐ coyote			
☐ desert iguana			
☐ desert tortoise			
☐ fox			
☐ golden eagle			
☐ ground squirrel			
☐ horned lizard			
☐ jackrabbit			
☐ kangaroo rat			
☐ mule deer			
☐ pocket gopher			
☐ quail			
☐ rattlesnake			
☐ raven			
☐ red-tailed hawk			
☐ roadrunner			
☐ tarantula			
☐ woodrat			
☐ _____			
☐ _____			
☐ _____			
☐ _____			
☐ _____			

Plants:	Date	Location	Observations
☐ barrel cactus			
☐ beavertail cactus			
☐ brittlebush			
☐ calico cactus			
☐ Canterberry bell			
☐ creosote bush			
☐ desert dandelion			
☐ globemallow			
☐ Joshua tree			
☐ Mojave yucca			
☐ mound cactus			
☐ palm tree			
☐ Parry nolina			
☐ pencil cholla			
☐ primrose			
☐ sand verbena			
☐ teddy bear cholla			
☐ _____			
☐ _____			
☐ _____			

Fun Things I Did:	Where	The best part about this was...
☐ took a hike		
☐ camped		
☐ had a picnic		
☐ went backpacking		
☐ drove Geology Tour Rd.		
☐ went to a ranger program		
☐ explored boulder piles		
☐ read roadside exhibits		
☐ identified plants		
☐ visited an historic site		
☐ stood on a mountain		
☐ watched rock climbers		
☐ looked for wildlife		

Places to Visit:	When	The best part about this was...
☐ Arch Rock		
☐ Barker Dam		
☐ Cap Rock		
☐ Cholla Cactus Garden		
☐ Cottonwood Spring		
☐ Covington Flats		
☐ Desert Queen Mine		
☐ Desert Queen Ranch		
☐ Eureka Peak		
☐ 49 Palms Oasis		
☐ Geology Tour Road		
☐ Headstone Rock		
☐ Hidden Valley		
☐ Indian Cove		
☐ Jumbo Rocks		
☐ Keys View		
☐ Lost Horse Mine		
☐ Lost Palms Oasis		
☐ Malipai Hill		
☐ Oasis of Mara		
☐ Oasis Visitor Center		
☐ Ocotillo Patch		
☐ Pinto Basin		
☐ Ryan Mountain		
☐ Skull Rock		
☐ Trojan		
☐ Wonderland of Rocks		

Ask a Ranger: Write down any questions you think of while exploring the park. Next time you see a ranger, find out the answer and record it here in your notes.

_____
_____
_____
_____

Answer Page

Fact Or Fiction: Explorer Thermometer

How many "Fact or Fiction" questions did you get right on your first guess? Compare your results with the Explorer Thermometer below. Which kind of Desert Explorer are you?

Correct Answers

Desert Genius — You have probably spent a great deal of time exploring or reading about Joshua Tree National Park and other deserts. You are still having fun because there is always more to explore and discover.

Desert Explorer — Either you have been to the park before or you are a good guesser. You found more to explore and discover, even as a repeat visitor. Of course, you found that learning about the desert is still fun.

Desert Rookie — This is probably your first visit to Joshua Tree National Park. You found much to explore and discover. The important thing is that you had fun.

Mini Mystery (*page 23*): 1). Shilo is a desert bighorn sheep. You can find information on bighorn sheep on pages 19 and 20. 2.) Like all desert bighorn sheep, Shilo prefers steep, rugged terrain. In the park, the Wonderland of Rocks (page 24) provides good rugged terrain for desert bighorn sheep. 3.) Desert bighorn sheep have sponge-like feet that help them climb over steep rocky terrain. 4.) The campers left the area after reading about day use areas. Bighorn sheep are shy and nervous. They will not come to the water hole while people are there. The campers did not want to keep animals like the bighorn from getting a drink of water.

Word Search Clues (page 39)

1. coyote
2. nolina
3. ground squirrel
4. Joshua tree
5. snakes
6. chuckwalla
7. tarantula
8. quail
9. datura
10. lion
11. barrel
12. tortoise

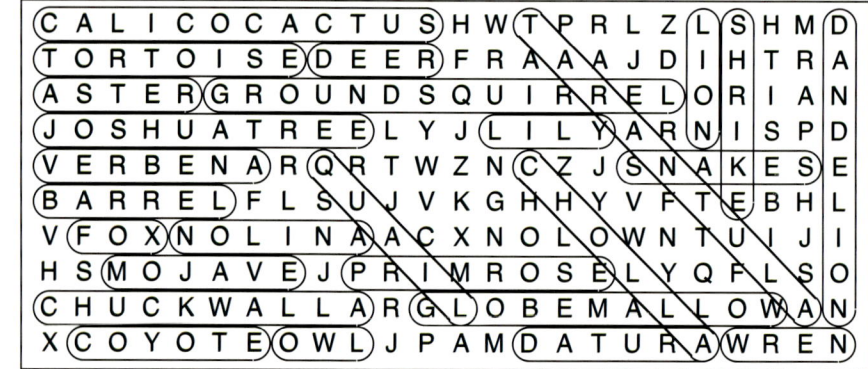

Crossword Puzzle (page 40)

Down
- 2. rat
- 4. beavertail
- 6. yucca
- 10. hike
- 11. jumping
- 13. ocotillo
- 15. horned
- 17. Keys

Across
- 1. Mormon
- 3. bobcat
- 5. Hoyt
- 7. Mara
- 8. Arch
- 9. orioles
- 11. jackrabbit
- 12. monzogranite
- 14. mortar
- 15. hawk
- 16. Colorado
- 18. roadrunner
- 19. lizard

My favorite scenic snapshot of Joshua Tree National Park

My favorite snapshot of me having fun at Joshua Tree National Park

JOSHUA TREE

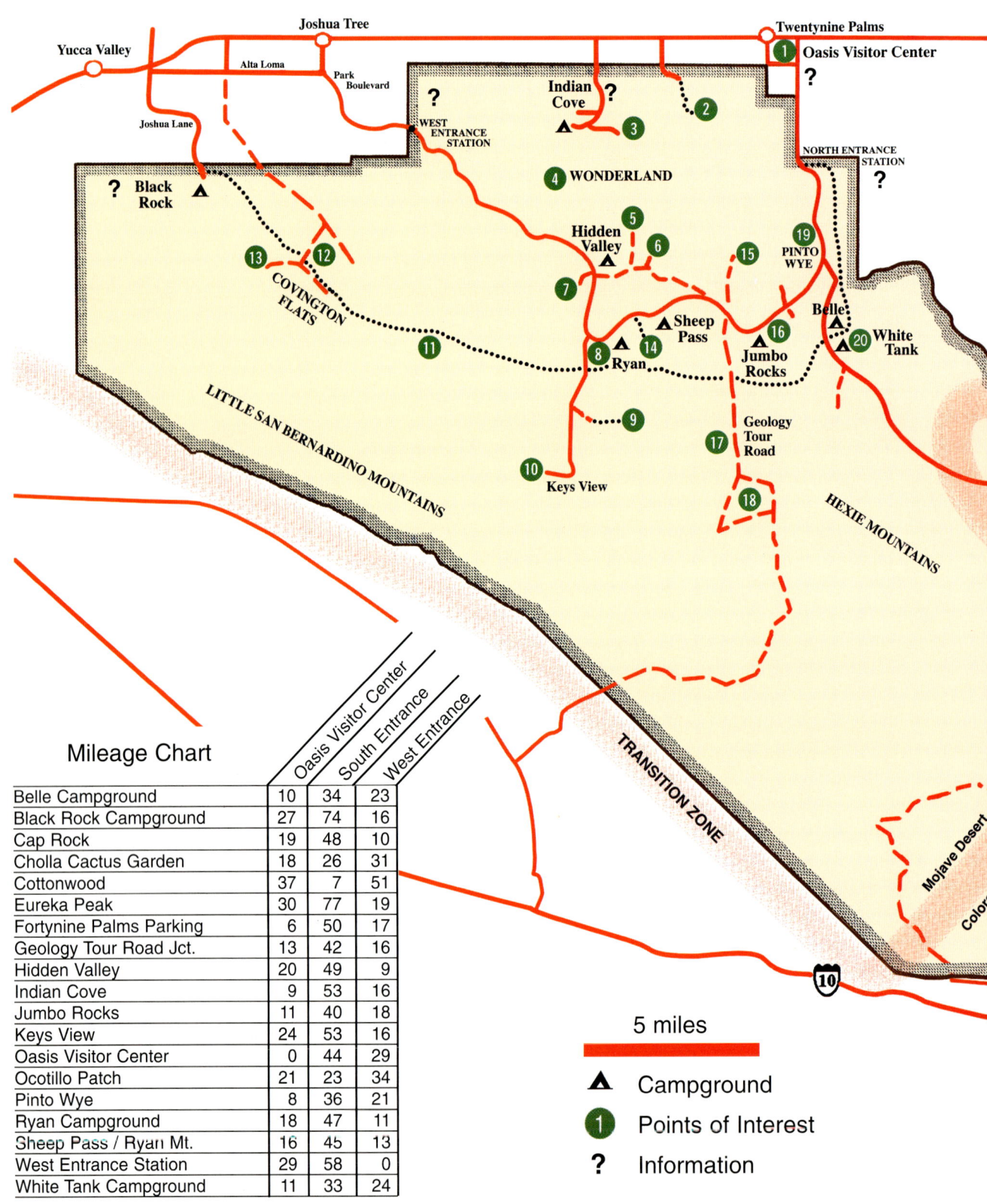

NATIONAL PARK

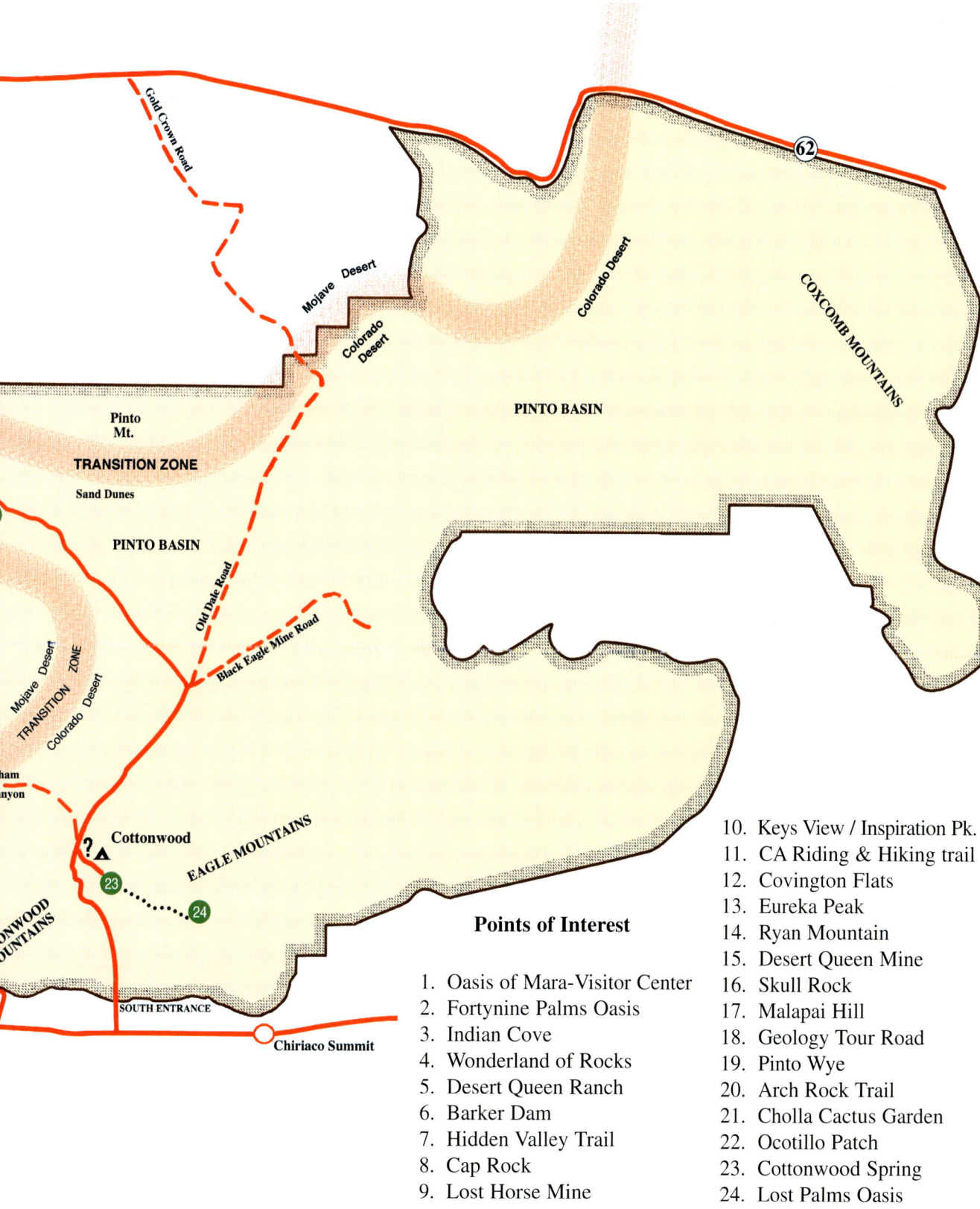

Points of Interest

1. Oasis of Mara-Visitor Center
2. Fortynine Palms Oasis
3. Indian Cove
4. Wonderland of Rocks
5. Desert Queen Ranch
6. Barker Dam
7. Hidden Valley Trail
8. Cap Rock
9. Lost Horse Mine
10. Keys View / Inspiration Pk.
11. CA Riding & Hiking trail
12. Covington Flats
13. Eureka Peak
14. Ryan Mountain
15. Desert Queen Mine
16. Skull Rock
17. Malapai Hill
18. Geology Tour Road
19. Pinto Wye
20. Arch Rock Trail
21. Cholla Cactus Garden
22. Ocotillo Patch
23. Cottonwood Spring
24. Lost Palms Oasis

Glossary: What Does That Word Mean?

adaptable - to be able to adjust or fit in to the surrounding environment
archaeologist - scientist who studies the remains of past human life
bird of prey - a bird who hunts live animals for food
camouflage - an animal's protective coloring that allows it to blend in with the surrounding environment
carrion - dead and decaying animals
dehydration - extreme loss of water from the body
hibernate - to spend a long time in a very deep sleep
metabolize - a chemical reaction in the body that breaks down substances (such as food) and creates substances necessary for life (such as water)
nocturnal - active at night
pollinate - to fertilize a plant with the powder (pollen) produced by a flowering plant
predator - an animal that hunts other animals for food
prey - an animal that is hunted or caught for food
rehydrate - to replenish a body's water supply
slot canyon - smooth, narrow canyon between solid rock cliffs

Index

Arch Rock, *27*, 35
Barker Dam, 24, 29, 30, 35
bighorn sheep, 19, *20*
bobcat, 18, *21*
cactus wren, 8
cactus
   barrel, 10, *11*
   beavertail, 9,*1 3*
   calico, 9, *13*
   cholla, 9, 10, *13*
   Mojave mound, 9, *13*
   old man, 9
   pancake, 9
   prickley pear, 9
CA Riding & Hiking trail, 35
Cap Rock, 26
Cholla Cactus Garden, 10
chuckwalla, *22*
Colorado Desert, *14*, 15
Covington Flats, *7*, 34
coyote, 18, *18*
Desert Queen Mine, 30

Desert Queen Ranch, 30, *31*
Eureka Peak, 34
fox, 18
Geology Tour Road, 26
ground squirrel, 18, *22*
hawk, red-tailed, 8, 18, *20*
Hidden Valley, 24, 25, 29, *36*
Hoyt, Minerva, 32
iguana, 18
jackrabbit, *21*
Joshua tree, 6, *6*, *7*, 9, 15
kangaroo rat, 18, 19
Keys, Bill, 30, 31
Keys View, 34
Indians, *see* Native Americans
Inspiration Peak, 35
lizard, 19
   chuckwalla, *22*
   horned, *19*
Lost Horse Mine, *30*, 35
Malapai Hill, 27
mesquite, 9, 15

Mojave Desert, *15*, 15
monzogranite, 24
mountain lion, *20*
Native Americans, 28 ,29
nolina, 10, *11*
oasis, 16
   Cottonwood Spring, 17, 29
   Fortynine Palms, 16, 35
   Lost Palms, 16, *17*, 35
   Twentynine Palms, Mara, 17
Oasis Visitor Center, 28, 34
Old Woman Rock, *4*, 25
ocotillo, 10, *12*, 15
oriole, 8
owl, 8
Pinto Basin, 26,
quail, *22*
rattlesnake, sidewinder, *21*
roadrunner, 18, 20 ,*21*
Ryan Mountain, 35
shrike, Loggerhead, 8
Skull Rock, 25

tarantula, *22*
toad, 18
tortoise, 19, *22*
Wall Street Mill, 30
wildflowers
   aster, 10, *11*
   Canterbury bells, 10, *13*
   dandelion, 10, *11*
   datura, 10, *12*
   desert lily, 10
   dune primrose, 10, *11*
   five-spot, 10
   globemallow, 10, *12*
   locoweed, 10
   Mariposa lily, 10, *12*
   phacelia, 10
   sand verbena, 10, *11*
woodpecker, 8
woodrat, 8
Wonderland, *24*
yucca, Mojave, 10, *12*
yucca moth, 7